AF427953

Elder Hammond and the Inspector

Elder Hammond and the Inspector

A Lesson in Faith, Persistence, and the Promise of Nephi

Bill Wylson

First Edition published April 2015
Second Edition published November 2024

White Horse Books
Green Stem Media

South Jordan, Utah

www.billwylsonbooks.com
www.greenstemmedia.com

- 4 -

"Writing is something you do alone.
It's a profession for introverts who
want to tell you a story but don't want
to make eye contact while doing it."

John Green

Elder Hammond and the Inspector

Table of Contents

Preface

"This is [a] blessing which hath been bestowed upon us, that we have been made instruments in the hands of God to bring about this great work." [1]

One of our Church's greatest missionaries, Elder LeGrand Richards, stated: "I have had many people ask me what my greatest church experience has been, and I un-hesitatingly say, 'My first mission! That is where I began to really love the Lord and His Church and

---

[1] Alma 26;3.

developed a desire to help build his Kingdom.'"

Like the tens of thousands of missionaries today bearing witness of the restored gospel of Jesus Christ, I was elated to be similarly engaged in a partnership with our heavenly Father in the great work of gathering Israel. I was privileged and honored to give my time and means to the establishment of His Kingdom on earth. And though my objective was to teach and serve others, I returned from my mission with a profound sense of personal growth and increased faith, devotion, and determination. I learned from personal experience that God can utilize His children, as young and immature as we are, as agents to accomplish His great work.

Among other things, I learned to depend on the Lord. I learned to pray with greater intensity and power and to be led and directed by the Spirit. And I discovered that God does answer our sincere, faith-filled prayers. Through my mission experiences, I learned to love the Lord with greater feelings and to love my fellow beings more fully, especially Elder Hammond, the farm boy from Kansas.

A lot has changed over the years: the manner in which missionaries teach and the names we use to refer to ourselves and the Church. The cities where I had served have grown and expanded, and the Church has expanded globally. Despite these facts, I believe that the message of this story remains as pertinent today as it was when Elder Hammond and I wandered the streets of Villa Mercedes, attempting to preach the gospel of Jesus Christ.

The events that I am about to relate to you actually occurred. In other words, they are true, sort of. I have attempted to retell them as accurately as my memory will permit. Names have been changed.

No book is published without the help of others, and I wish to thank, sincerely and in random order, all those who have helped make this book possible: Bertha Didley, Oldone Jimenez, Monica Foston, Donald Pibcolo, Merle Umre, and Lawrence Klingensmith. These individuals played significant roles in my missionary journey, and I am deeply grateful for their contributions. Of course, these names have also been changed, so it does little good to mention them at all. (You know who you are!)

I also thank my sweet wife, who patiently plays the part of the poor widow while I lock myself in my office to recount my tales and adventures. Her unwavering support and understanding have been invaluable, and I am deeply grateful for her presence in my life.

"It is our duty, divinely imposed, to continue urgently and militantly to carry forward our missionary work. We must continue to call missionaries and send them out to preach the gospel, which was never more needed than now, which is the only remedy for the tragic ills that now afflict the world, and which alone can bring peace and brotherly love back amongst the peoples of the earth." [2]

---

[2] The First Presidency of the Church Jesus Christ of Latter-day Saints.

Elder Hammond and the Inspector

The Villa Mercedes District

The sweet-scented odor of autumn rose from the withered leaves that swirled around our scuffed and worn shoes. I tightened my London Fog overcoat against a chilling pre-wintry gust.

"What's that thing they say about God?" I asked Elder Hammond as we slowly shuffled—well, as I shuffled, Hammond sort of galumphed—through *Plaza Pedernera* in the center of town. Hammond was more the galumphing type.

"What thing?" he asked.

"You know," I elaborated. "That thing...

...that they say...

...about God."

"Do you mean that 'God works in mysterious ways?'"

"Precisely, Hammond!"

They say that God works in mysterious ways, which is just another way of saying, "I don't understand what God is up to." In my brief and puerile twenty-one years on this planet, I have seen some of the mysterious ways of God and the resultant miracles that follow. Still, whatever God was up to in the small town of Villa Mercedes was definitely a mystery to all of us.

Two weeks prior to my walking through *Plaza Pedernera*, I was serving as the District Leader in the city of Mendoza, with barely two months left before my mission ended. Transfers had already been announced about a month earlier, and my name was missing from the list. It seemed apparent that I would finish my mission in Mendoza. But then the phone rang.

"Hello."

"Elder Wylson?" a voice asked. "This is Elder Stevens, Assistant to the President."

Elder Stevens was not only the Assistant to the Mission President, but he and I also started our missions on the same day. We had spent two months together in the Mission Training Center, but our paths hadn't crossed since then. During our time in the MTC, Stevens was laid back and easygoing. He lived in a languid mellowness reminiscent of a washed-out hippie. He probably *was* a washed-out hippie, but now, as Assistant to the President, he had become, well, let's say, a little more militant in his demeanor. Rumor had it he was known as Sergeant Stevens around the halls of the mission home.

"Oh. Hey, how you doin'?" I asked amicably.

"No time to twaddle. You need to pack your things immediately," Stevens continued, "and purchase a bus ticket to Villa Mercedes. Elder Bowen will be replacing you. Your new companion will be Elder Hammond."

"Hammond?" I questioned. "I thought he was up north in Salta or someplace."

"Not anymore. He left a couple of days ago. You need to be in Villa Mercedes by tomorrow."

"Well, hold on a second. Elder Hammond started his mission the same day you and I did."

"That's right," Stevens answered abruptly.

"So, we'll both be going home in two months. Both at the same time."

"Yes. Be sure you get to Villa Mercedes by tomorrow. They're expecting you."

With that, Elder Stevens hung up the phone, leaving me to wonder why the Mission President would put two missionaries together who would both be going home at the same time and in the not-too-distant future. I turned to my companion, Elder Kirk.

"Guess what. I'm being transferred to Villa Mercedes tomorrow."

"Really?"

"Yeah. Elder Bowen will be your new companion, but do you know what's strange?" I asked.

"People who don't like *dulce de leche*?"

I looked disapprovingly at Elder Kirk as he smeared another glop of the gooey, sweet caramel on his half-eaten banana.

"Do you eat that stuff on everything?" I asked

"Pretty much."

"Well, what's strange is my new companion is Elder Hammond. What about corn on the cob?"

"Corn on the cob? Yeah. I've had it on that, too. So, what's strange about Elder Hammond?"

"A lot of things, if I remember correctly, but principally, he and I are both going home in two months."

"So?" replied Elder Kirk, failing to grasp the dire severity of this perplexing situation.

"So, normally we get transferred every four to six months, right?"

"Right."

"If both Hammond and I are going home in two months, then one of us will have to be transferred again in about six weeks so a replacement can be trained. What about steak?" I asked, still watching him devour his *dulce de leche*.

"Yeah, I've had it on steak, too."

"That's disgusting!"

"Listen, I'm sure the Mission President knows what he's doing, putting you and Elder Hammond together," replied Elder Kirk.

"I'm not so sure. It simply makes no sense. No sense at all."

It was, in fact, just the beginning of things that made no sense.

I arrived in Villa Mercedes the following afternoon. It is a small town located near the banks of the *Quinto* River and nestled in the southern foothills of *Sierra del Yulto* in the province of San Luis, Argentina. The city was founded around December 1st, 1856, as a mixed civilian-military fort known as *Fortín Constitucional* in an effort to protect the territory against attacks by the *Ranquel* aboriginal tribes. Its original name was changed in 1861 to Villa Mercedes after its residents adopted the Virgin of Mercy (*Virgen de las Mercedes*) as their patron.

Villa Mercedes proliferated after a railway line reached the town in 1875 and was officially declared a city in 1896. Water for irrigation from the *Quinto* River enabled the area to become an important grain and cattle-producing region. Anyone who has been there can tell you that Argentine beef is the best. Why someone would put *dulce de leche* on it is beyond me!

When I arrived in Villa Mercedes, Elders Price and Phillips met me at the bus station. They must have checked the schedule for buses coming in from Mendoza and suspected I'd arrive when I did. Elder Price was the District Leader and still had eight months left before completing his mission. He and I had served together when I was the Zone Leader in San Rafael.

You had to feel sorry for Elder Price. When I first met him, he was relatively new to the mission field. One afternoon, he was reading the conference issue of the *Ensign* magazine when he noticed that one of the crowd pictures was a photograph of his girlfriend sitting on a bench in Temple Square with another guy.

His countenance dropped dramatically.

"Could be anyone," I reassured him. "Could be her brother."

"Her brothers are younger than her, younger than this guy anyway!"

"Well, a cousin then," I offered.

"It's not her cousin."

"Maybe it's just someone who sat down to ask her where the nearest drinking fountain might be. Nothing to worry about."

Price found my reassurances less than reassuring and refused to be swayed from his suspicions that while the cat was away, the mouse, as it were, was attending General Conference with a nefarious character attempting to steal away Price's girlfriend. He immediately wrote to her demanding to know what was going on. Two weeks later he received her answer in the form of a 'Dear John' letter explaining that the man sitting next to her in the photograph was her new fiancée. Elder Price was heartbroken and devastated. As I said, you just had to pity the poor guy.

What surprised me was Elder Phillips was also in Villa Mercedes. Elder Phillips and I had started our missions together with Elder Hammond in the Mission Training Center. Consequently, all three of us would be going home on the same day.

"Are we the only four missionaries in Villa Mercedes?" I asked. "Because it looks like three of us are going home in two months."

"No, there are two Sister Missionaries here as well: Sister Rogers and Sister Campbell," Elder Phillips reassured me. "They both arrived yesterday. They are replacing the two Elders who were here before I arrived."

"Well, that's encouraging," I said.

"Not really," Elder Price added. "They're also both going home in two months. In fact, they leave the same day that you, Hammond, and Phillips do."

I was feeling nonplussed.

"Are you kidding me?" I blurted out. To say that it perplexed me to no end would be an understatement. "There are six missionaries here and five of us are going home in two months? That means that half the district will have to be transferred in six weeks so that replacement missionaries can be trained."

"Looks that way," said Elder Phillips.

Elder Phillips was from Bakersfield, California. There seemed to exist a kind of acrimony, if that's the word I'm looking for, between the missionaries from California and the missionaries from Utah. A saying circulated through the mission fields that missionaries from California went on missions to share their testimony, while missionaries from Utah went on missions to gain a testimony.

My father served as Mission President once, and I asked him about it. He told me that he had heard similar speculations. He also told me that when a situation arose, the missionaries he could always count on were the ones from Utah.

In our little District of thirteen Elders at the Mission Training Center, five were from Utah, and four were from California. There was also one germophobic vegetarian from Boston and a half cowboy—half city slicker type from Arizona. I had left for my mission from Chicago, but while I was still in the MTC, my family moved to Los Angeles. Elder Phillips was the first to accept me as a California missionary. He and I quickly became friends, and I was happy to learn that we were finishing our missions in the same area.

The last of our little group of thirteen was Elder Hammond, a freckled-face, shy sort of bumpkin from some little farm town in Kansas. He was awkward and withdrawn. Even in his white shirt and tie, he reminded me of the kind of kid you'd see in denim coveralls, wearin' a straw hat and chompin' on a thin blade of grass whilst irrigatin' the lower forty. He was a bit of a Hogs-Norton, if that's the phrase I'm looking for, uncultured and boorish, who knew little about the rules and mannerisms of normal society.

He never spoke much while we were at the MTC, so I knew very little about him. That would all change very shortly. I turned to Elder Price.

"So, where's my companion now?" I inquired.

"Oh, he's back at the apartment."

"Seriously?" I asked.

"Yes. Quite seriously."

"You know, there's a word to describe someone who won't even bother to come meet his new companion at the bus station. It starts with an 'O' or, I don't know, maybe a 'C' or something."

"He said he wanted to stay at the apartment and study his scriptures," added Elder Phillips.

"I think it's 'C-a—... No, I've lost it. Oh, well, doesn't matter."

Elder Price and Elder Phillips escorted me to my new apartment, a small home owned by an elderly woman who rented out a room to missionaries. Before leaving, Elder Price asked me to remind Elder Hammond that we'd be holding a missionary District meeting at the chapel at six o'clock.

I went inside to find Elder Hammond stretched out across his bed, dutifully immersed in his study of the scriptures.

"Ah, so you've arrived." Apparently, Elder Hammond has a real knack for grasping the obvious.

"Yes, I have," I responded.

"Well, that bed there is yours," he drawled, pointing to the only other bed in the room on which he wasn't already sprawling. I set my suitcase on the mattress and began to unpack. Under normal circumstances, this would be the time when new companions become better acquainted with each other, but Elder Hammond seemed content to go on studying. He was reading one of Paul's epistles and copying verses onto the back of business cards with a blue pen.

Since Elder Hammond kept his nose firmly embedded in the New Testament, and since I, quite frankly, could think of nothing to say anyway, I unpacked in silence. When my things were all put away, I sat on the bed.

"Oh, um, by the way," I announced. "Elder Price wanted me to remind you of the District meeting this evening."

"Uh-huh," responded my reticent new companion, his eyes still fixated on the writings of Paul.

"So, what are you doing with those cards?" I asked with the distinct feeling that I was interrupting something exceptionally significant.

"What? These?" he replied, holding up the card he had just finished writing on.

I refrained from saying, "Yes, those, since those are the only cards you seem to be doing anything with at the moment." Instead, I simply said, "Yes."

"Oh. These. Well, these are my scripture cards."

I was waiting for further explanation, but none was forthcoming, so I bravely delved deeper.

"So, what are you doing with them?"

"Well, I'm writing on them," he informed me, and then, sensing that I may need additional enlightenment, he added, "I'm writing scriptures on them."

"Why?" I patiently inquired.

"So they'll fit in my shirt pocket."

"Oh," I replied, still bewildered. "Why do you want to fit them in your pocket?"

"I carry them in my pocket so I can take them out and re-read them."

"Oh," I replied again. "And why do you do that?"

"Well, that's how I memorize them."

"You're memorizing the New Testament?" I asked, raising my eyebrows in astonishment.

"Of course not! Don't be ridiculous. Just the epistles of Paul."

"Really?" I responded.

"Yeah. I love the writings of Paul. He was the greatest missionary of all time."

Elder Hammond grabbed another card and continued his little exercise. I paused briefly before continuing our conversation.

"What do you suppose is going to happen," I asked, "in a month or so?"

"What do you mean?" he responded— again without looking up.

"Well, I'm guessing one of us will have to be transferred again so the other can train a new companion."

"I guess so," he casually commented.

"It seems a bit odd, don't you think? I mean, five of us going home all on the same day? The Mission President will have to replace half of us at least a couple of weeks before that. It just seems a bit peculiar."

"Oh, I dunno."

At least Elder Hammond did not cloud our conversation with frivolous talk that was not of the essence.

"What about contacts?" I asked.

"Contacts?" Elder Hammond responded as he copied another verse from Paul.

"Yeah, I mean, are we teaching anyone?"

"Well, I got here two nights ago and spent the day with Elder Kocherhans, he's the guy you replaced."

"Okay."

"Well, he spent most of the day yesterday packing and saying good-bye to the members and then he left for Tucumán," Elder Hammond informed me.

"And did he introduce you to any of the families that he was teaching?"

"No. He said we didn't have any."

"No one?" I asked, surprised.

"Pretty much," Hammond responded. "Kocherhans said they spent most of their time knocking on doors."

"Is that all?"

"No. He also said they weren't very good at it."

As we apparently had nothing planned for that afternoon and Elder Hammond seemed content to sprawl on his bed reading and copying the scriptures, I laid back on my mattress and spent the rest of the afternoon contemplating the infinite through the inside of my eyelids. I believe it was Shakespeare himself who first referred to sleep as 'nature's sweet restorer,' and a little restoration never hurt anyone.

The District meeting began promptly at quarter past six due to the Sisters being late. We started the meeting by brutally murdering W. W. Phelps' hymn, *Redeemer of Israel* a Capello, followed by a prayer from Elder Phillips. Elder Price then stood to introduce and welcome the new missionaries, which was basically everyone but him. He then commenced enthusiastically extolling the Mission President's exceptional and inspired insight in placing the most experienced missionaries together in one tiny village.

"Like all of you, I've been wondering why the Mission President would assign missionaries to Villa Mercedes who are all going home so soon. It occurred to me that this is one of the most extraordinary things I have seen on my mission. Just think about it! Think of the spiritual strength that all of you bring to the district!" he unashamedly blandished. "You are the best of the best, the most experienced missionaries in the entire mission. Just think of it," he repeated. "God can work mighty miracles here through you."

The effervescence of his enthusiasm was astonishing. It was a bubbly viewpoint to which I did not adhere.

"I dunno," I countered. "Maybe the Mission President thought we'd all get too trunky and homesick and didn't want us infecting the rest of the mission field."

For those of you who are unfamiliar with missionary jargon, a trunky missionary is a missionary who is overly anxious to return home to, shall we say, normal life? He or she packs his or her trunk months before their release date and thinks primarily not of missionary work but of whatever lies ahead in the real world back home.

"Oh, I don't think so," replied Elder Price, still wholeheartedly fervent and enthusiastic despite my indifference. "I believe the Mission President knew exactly what he was doing. We will see miracles occur in the next two months. So, I want to challenge all of you to not dwell on what's going to happen just down the road, but to focus on the work at hand and remember, above all else, that you are all disciples of Christ."

"Well, I don't know about that!" I interjected.

"You don't know about what?" asked Elder Price.

"I think we're rather likeable, both the guys and the gals."

"What are you talking about?"

"You said, we're all dislikeable guys and I was just pointing out that—"

"I never said any such thing!" Elder Price insisted.

"Well, then what did you say?" I asked.

"I said, you are all disciples of Christ."

"Oh. Well, that certainly makes more sense than what you said before."

"I never said—you know what, just forget it." He appeared somewhat agitated by our conversation for some reason. "I believe this is an inspired strategy on the President's part to set this town on fire."

I'm sure he meant 'set on fire' spiritually and not literally, but even after such a rousing speech, I was still skeptical. I have always had a somewhat cynical mind. I believe that God can and does perform miracles, but in my case, I wonder why He would. So, I pray. I study my scriptures. I follow the mission rules most of the time, sort of. And I have been a successful missionary. I don't assume credit for the conversions I played a part in, as that is the exclusive role of the Holy Ghost. I recognize that, but I have participated in teaching and baptizing numerous families in the months I have served.

None of this, however, occurred under what I'd consider miraculous circumstances. My companions and I did the work and were blessed with the results. I'm confident angels were behind the scenes orchestrating our success, but, on the surface, we were just a couple of inexperienced and somewhat immature boys moving blindly about the vital business of gathering Israel.

Of course, you never know when a miracle may be waiting for you just around the corner... and I mean that literally.

The Inspector

Two weeks had passed since my arrival when Elder Hammond and I found ourselves shuffling through *Plaza Pedernera* on that chilly late-autumn afternoon. The cold wind swirled dry fallen leaves around our shoes, carrying with it a bitter sting that warned of the coming winter.

Villa Mercedes, nestled amidst woodlands and grasslands perfect for bovine pasture, is a sight to behold. Its main roads, few and far between, are paved, while most of its streets are cobblestone or dirt, flanked by majestic Jacaranda trees.

You would have to see the stunning beauty of the Jacaranda in full bloom to truly appreciate its exquisiteness. The slender trunk, delicate leaves, and rich lilac blossoms make it an object of spotless splendor. If I had to describe the beauty of the Jacaranda in just one word, I would say it is breath-taking, which is actually two words but neither breath nor taking by themselves provide an adequate description.

The amazing purple blooms of spring transition to rich, yellow hues in the fall, making the Jacaranda a prominent beauty season-to-season. Fernlike foliage lends volume to its bold, dramatic silhouette for a characteristically classic look that is awe-inspiring, which is also two words.

Deep color emerges as a sea of lavender decorates the tree, making the arbor strikingly artful. Large, silky flowers hang in heavy, full bunches, ushering in the summer season. Walking along a street lined with Jacarandas is an ethereal experience. The Jacaranda's silhouette is even more magnificent when those bold blossoms give way to golden autumnal tones. Eye-catching is a word that comes to mind.

Maybe it would have been easier to come up with a single word to describe the Jacaranda's splendor if Elder Hammond and I hadn't been serving here at the beginning of the winter months. The trees had dropped their leaves, the air was filled with a cold chill, and the usually warm and inviting people I care for so deeply seemed as uninviting and cold as the approaching winter winds.

At the center of *Plaza Pedernera* stands a statue of Juan Pedernera on horseback. The plaza was named for Juan Esteban Pedernera, who was born in San Luis on Christmas day in 1796 and briefly served as interim President of Argentina in 1861.

As a boy, Pedernera studied in a Franciscan monastery but left to join the Regiment of Mounted Grenadiers after being summoned by General San Martín to fight in the War of Independence against Spanish rule. The Spanish captured and imprisoned him, but he managed to escape and rejoin his army.

He joined the Unitarian side in the Argentine Civil War and fought against federalist forces in *La Tablada*. In 1856, he was designated commander of the frontier armed forces, and in 1859, he was elected Governor of San Luis.

He was later elected Vice President to the President of the Argentine Confederation, Santiago Derqui. When Derqui resigned after the Battle of *Pavón*, Pedernera acted as President until the political situation forced the dissolution of the office. In 1882, he was designated Lieutenant General of the Armies of the Republic.

So, it is only fitting for this brave and admirable man to have a plaza named after him, and while *Plaza Pedernera* is central to the town of Villa Mercedes, it is not central to this story. Hammond and I were less than enthusiastic as we lumbered through the plaza that fateful afternoon. In the past two weeks, we had had no success, had made no important contacts, and had nothing to do but knock on doors, an activity that any missionary would find disheartening, to say the least.

At three in the afternoon, the streets of Villa Mercedes were silent and empty—barren is a word that comes to mind—lacking the usual bustling populace. This was due to the afternoon practice of *siesta*. Taking an extended lunch break, including a nap, is common in several Mediterranean, tropical, and subtropical countries, but a *siesta* is more than just a short nap taken in the early afternoon.

In Argentina, all government offices and businesses, shops and markets, museums and churches close at lunch and remain closed until three-thirty or four in the afternoon so that proprietors can go home for a long lunch and a snooze.

The commendable practice of taking a *siesta* is like a tonic to the soul. Studies indicate that those who nap have less risk of heart attack. The *siesta* habit has been associated with a thirty-seven percent reduction in coronary mortality, possibly due to reduced cardiovascular stress mediated by daytime sleep.

It was the poet Ogden Nash, I believe, who wrote that "no man is greater than his respect for sleep," and Shakespeare himself tells us that "sleep knits up the raveled sleeve of care." The possibility of me ever becoming even an interim president of Argentina is, well, nil at best, but if it were ever to happen, my first act as Supreme Ruler would be to remove all the statues of the great military leaders of South America, like General San Martin and Juan Esteban Pedernera and replace them with a statue of whoever first came up with the concept of the *siesta*.

"To sleep:" writes the Bard, "perchance to dream: ay, there's the rub." After a couple of solid hours of shut-eye immediately following lunch, the world seems a better place. Sunlight guilds the treetops, and little birds chirp and twitter. Of course, they do that whether you've had a *siesta* or not, but they are distinctly more appreciated when you have had one. Missionaries, of course, are encouraged to use this time to study the scriptures or learn the missionary discussions.

It would be another half an hour before the *siesta* officially ended, and the small town would begin to show signs of life again. So far, none of the missionary companionships in Villa Mercedes had set the town on fire.

Elder Hammond and I spent our first few days introducing ourselves to some of the members. We had knocked on doors looking for that special family who had been simply waiting for us to show up on their doorstep and invite them into the waters of baptism. Elders Price and Phillips were teaching a college-aged young lady who showed more interest in the missionaries than in their message, as is often the case with college-aged young ladies. The closest any of us came to even creating a spark of success were the Sister Missionaries, who were teaching a young family. All hope for a convert baptism within the remaining few weeks ahead was on them.

Villa Mercedes is home to approximately 50,000 residents. As Elder Hammond and I left the plaza and crossed the street heading east, 49,999 of those residents were still deeply submerged in the throes of their *siesta*. We did, however, notice one solitary individual wandering the streets, an elderly man in a trench coat and hat. The old gentleman stopped to gaze in the occasional shop window as he slowly toddled toward us. Elder Hammond leaned in and whispered to me.

"You see that guy?" he asked.

"Yes," I said. "What about him?"

"Don't you think that guy looks like Inspector Clouseau?" he responded, garnishing a boyish grin that perfectly resembled the look of a fourth-grade scamp who had just shared a bit of potty humor with a fellow classmate.

I was quite taken aback by Elder Hammond's declaration. First and foremost, I was stunned to discover that Elder Hammond had a sense of humor. Up until this very moment in our companionship, he had seemed only sullen, serious, and spiritual. Secondly, it surprised me that anyone would think this portly old man looked anything at all like Inspector Clouseau. The Pink Panther movies have always been favorites of mine. In fact, the last movie I saw before going on my mission was *The Return of the Pink Panther*, and this elderly gentleman looked nothing like the character portrayed by Peter Sellers.

I was about to mention this to my misguided and immensely mistaken companion when he leaned in again and, almost as if he had read my thoughts, whispered: "Not the one from the movies, I mean the one from the cartoons."

This caused me to pause. I had to admit he had something there. The old fellow did seem to resemble the cartoon version of Inspector Clouseau. He was short and stout, sporting a similar mustache, and, with his trench coat and hat, actually bore a striking resemblance to the cartoon detective. I began to grin a little myself.

Clearing my throat, I quoted, in my best Clouseau accent, "Ere ess a-luking at yew, keed." This caused both of us to chortle a touch under our breaths. It also caused Inspector Clouseau to look up. Smiling, perhaps a little too much, we greeted him with a friendly "Good Afternoon" as we walked passed him.

"Good afternoon, Elders," he replied.

Now you see, here is where you have to admire a simple country bumpkin like Elder

Hammond. Most of the population in Argentina refer to the LDS missionaries as *Mormones, Yanquis, Americanos,* or, occasionally, something indicating dislike or disdain. Once in a rare while, a few of them will employ the kinder term, *Hermanos.* But the old Inspector had just referred to us by our proper Priesthood title. This rarely happens outside of the Church.

Admittedly, it hadn't even registered with me, but Elder Hammond picked up on it right away. Turning abruptly around, he responded:

"Oh, so you know who we are?"

"Of course," replied the Inspector. You're the Mormon missionaries. You meet in the little Church just across from the plaza."

"Have you ever attended one of our meetings?" asked Elder Hammond.

"Several years ago, yes."

"We would love to come by your house and talk to you some more about our religion," Elder Hammond stated as he reached into his inside suitcoat pocket for his grey planner and blue ink pen. "Will you be home tomorrow evening, or would Saturday be better for you?"

"Yes. Tomorrow would be fine."

"At about 6:30?"

"*Bien*," replied the Inspector.

Elder Hammond noted the Inspector's name and address and jotted down the appointment for Thursday at 6:30 p.m.

"Then we will see you tomorrow evening," stated Elder Hammond. The Inspector then returned to his gongoozling while Elder Hammond and I continued walking toward an unproductive and ineffective afternoon of knocking on doors.

"This guy is golden," exclaimed Elder Hammond when we were out of earshot. "I can just feel it!"

If you were ever to read down my exceptionally long list of pet peeves, you would eventually come to one that reads: "I hate it when missionaries refer to their contacts as golden." We had barely met this man. We honestly had no idea what his interest in the

Church might be. Occasionally, we'd meet someone who just wants to practice their English skills. Other times, we'd run into someone who simply wanted to learn more about the United States and our customs. Sometimes, people who have no interest in the Church are just trying to be polite by not turning us away.

Granted, as I mentioned earlier, I tend to be a little more skeptical than most, but I had to wonder, if the Inspector had attended our Church at one point, why had he stopped going? Certainly, there had to have been some, or even several, devoutly faithful and devoted missionaries working closely with him in the past who prayerfully yet unsuccessfully attempted to get him to enter the waters of baptism. They had possibly even written in their missionary journals how he was their golden contact, and yet, Elder Hammond and I had found the Inspector walking the streets of Villa Mercedes still unpersuaded, unconverted, and unbaptized. There had to be something amiss.

I turned my collar up against the cold breeze that blew.

"Yup, Elder Wylson," Hammond reiterated. "This guy is golden!"

Thursday evening could not arrive soon enough for Elder Hammond. Not wishing to present myself as a missionary who lacked faith in the miraculous and wonderous powers of Heaven, and because I really didn't have anything else planned for Thursday evening, I figured I would go along with my good companion to buoy him up in the face of bitter disappointment as the Inspector unloaded on us his reasons for not joining the Church of Jesus Christ of Latter-day Saints previously. Also, I had to go. After all, we were inseparable companions.

The address the Inspector gave us was close to where we had met him the day before. His modest home butted up against a sidewalk lined with eye-catching and awe-inspiring Jacaranda trees. A stoop consisting of three cement steps led up to a massive wooden door. I climbed the three steps and pounded forcibly on the massive door but to no avail. No one answered.

Immediately, my skeptical disposition took over. "I knew it!" I told myself. "The old codger gave us the slip." Not infrequently, when a missionary meets a stranger on the street and requests to be invited to their home for a discussion on why they should change their religion and basically their entire lifestyle, the stranger will, for reasons we can only imagine, give a false address. Or, they may provide the correct address but conveniently make other plans outside of the home at the time of the scheduled visit. But ever the persistent one, I pounded upon the door a second time.

Still no response.

I turned and descended the three steps.

"Looks like the Inspector gave us a fake address or lied to us about bein' home tonight," I told my companion. But even in the face of inarguable evidence indicating that no one was present at this particular residence at this particular time, Elder Hammond ascended the steps and banged on the door a third time.

Surprisingly, the door swung wide open to reveal a tiny elderly woman with the look of a ferocious, untamed lioness eyeing two slabs of raw meat. She glared crossly at both of us and then, without a word, slammed the door shut.

Grateful to have not been eaten alive, I said to Elder Hammond, "Well, that, I guess, is that. Looks like the Inspector is not really interested in hearing our message."

It appeared I had sized up the situation somewhat precisely. To say I was disappointed would be a prevarication of the truth. I felt a sort of sick satisfaction in being right about the Inspector's aforementioned reluctance to join the Church. But then, these types of deep insights came somewhat naturally to me. You wouldn't expect a chump from Kansas to have the same keen awareness of mind as you would of, for example, a young man from Chicago. But Hammond, explicitly ignoring my superior insight, pounded robustly against the massive wooden door for the fourth time, and once again, the door swung open.

Expecting to see the same tiny elderly woman, this time brandishing a rolling pin, broom handle, or umbrella, I was stunned and, well, bowled-over is a word that comes to mind, when the Inspector himself stood in the doorway and politely beckoned us to enter his home. I entered the house behind Elder Hammond, cautiously keeping an eye out for a rolling pin-wielding woman who might have it in for us. The coast, however, was clear.

The Inspector led us directly into his office and prudently pulled the door shut. He invited us to sit in the two chairs on the opposite side of his desk. The large desk, too large for the size of the office, was made of a rich mahogany. A matching credenza and bookcase filled the rest of the room.

"I wish to apologize for my wife," pleaded the Inspector. "She has a religion of her own already."

We assured him that her behavior was completely understandable and acceptable, although none of us actually thought so. We quickly changed the subject by voicing our admiration for his fine mahogany desk with matching credenza and bookcase. This seemed to please him considerably, and after several minutes of phatic spackle and polite small talk, we began our discussion of holier matters.

We teach six discussions as missionaries, usually in a particular order. There is also a baptismal challenge that can be addressed at any appropriate moment as the Spirit indicates. The first of the six discussions begins with the story of Joseph Smith.

I initiated the discussion, elaborating on the perplexing circumstances that young Joseph found himself tackling regarding the "great clash in religious sentiment," which "created no small stir and division amongst the people, some crying, 'Lo, here!' and others, 'Lo, there!'" when the Inspector abruptly announced: "Oh, I already know all about Joseph Smith."

"You do?" I asked, somewhat puzzled and perplexed. Well, mystified, one might say.

"Yes. I do," he replied, opening a substantial drawer in his substantial desk and removing a copy of the Joseph Smith pamphlet. It was a much older version than the one we were currently distributing, but it was, nonetheless, an official Church publication. As curious and odd as this was, it was curiouser, if that's even a word, and odder to see that the Inspector's desk drawer was filled with a significant number of what appeared to be old Church literature and pamphlets. Apparently, missionaries had been visiting the Inspector often over the past several years.

Looking at the Joseph Smith pamphlet, I asked: "Have you read this?"

"Yes, of course," replied the Inspector.

"And do you believe what Joseph Smith relates in that story?"

"Absolutely, I do."

I can't say I knew what was happening in Elder Hammond's bucolic mind, but I thought I could almost sense his taunting words pounding relentlessly against my tympanic membrane: "Golden contact! Golden contact! Golden contact!"

"Well, then you must also know about the Book of Mormon," I remarked.

"Yes, of course." The Inspector stood up, reached down a book from his large mahogany bookcase, and showed us his personal copy of the Book of Mormon.

"So, have you read any of it?" I asked.

"Yes, I've read it twice."

"What?"

"I've read it twice."

"Twice?" I asked.

"Yes, twice. Oh, and I also read this other book." The Inspector stood again, this time reaching down a copy of the Doctrine and Covenants.

"You've read the Doctrine and Covenants as well?" I asked.

"Yes," he replied

"All of it?" I asked in disbelief.

"Yes, all of it."

I hadn't even read the Doctrine and Covenants myself at that time. Sure, I had read passages and sections, but not the entire book cover-to-cover like the Inspector claims to have done.

"So how long have you known about the Church?" Elder Hammond asked.

"I met the missionaries for the first time about—" he paused, looking upward for a moment— "twenty years ago, more or less."

"And you say you've attended our services before?" I inquired.

"Yes, I have gone to your Church on several occasions."

"Then do you know about the Plan of Salvation?" I asked.

"The Plan of Salvation? No. What is that?"

"Ah-ha!" I thought to myself. "Here's a subject we can actually teach him something about."

The second discussion covers the Plan of Salvation, and I let Elder Hammond take the lead on this one. We spent the better part of the next hour talking about the Lord's Plan of Salvation, or Plan of Happiness. We discovered that the Inspector knew all about it from previous discussions with other missionaries; he just didn't realize it is called 'The Plan of Salvation.'

We ended our discussion with a prayer, invited the Inspector to Church services on Sunday, and set an appointment to come back the following week. The Inspector showed us to the massive door, and as we headed back toward our apartment, Elder Hammond exclaimed, "This guy is golden, Elder Wylson! I told ya', this guy is golden!"

I still had my doubts.

Over the next couple of weeks, we visited the Inspector several times. I must admit I enjoyed sharing the gospel message with someone genuinely interested in learning everything we could teach him.

As we reported our progress in District meetings, everyone in the District became acquainted with the Inspector. None of us ever called him by his actual name. From the first moment we saw him on the street, he was 'The Inspector.' Elder Hammond optimistically talked about the great progress we were making in our discussions with him. Mostly, I refrained from voicing my concerns that if the man had wanted to be baptized, he would have done so by now. We continued inviting him to attend Church services with us, but he hadn't yet made an appearance. Elder Hammond had asked him to invite his wife to join us in our discussions at their home, but the Inspector insisted his wife would not be interested.

Elders Price and Phillips continued to teach the college-aged young lady but failed to enlist her commitment to attend Church or be baptized. The Sister Missionaries made the disappointing announcement that they had stopped by to teach the fourth discussion to their golden family but that the father had refused to let them enter his home.

"There is a strange feeling in our house when you're here," the gentleman explained to them.

"That feeling," Sister Campbell clarified, "is the Holy Spirit testifying to you that our message is from God."

But the feeling was too unfamiliar and enigmatic for this poor fellow and his family, so he closed his doors to the Sister Missionaries, inviting them not to return.

It now seemed that the Inspector was the most likely prospect for joining the Church in all of Villa Mercedes, but I could not see him making any commitment beyond what he had already done.

I had to concede that he was one of the most well-read and well-versed non-members I had ever met. He seemed genuinely interested in the gospel and participated very actively in our discussions. He knew the doctrine as well as any missionary, which, admittedly, isn't much. Still, it was exceptionally more than most investigators we encountered on the streets. We continued to visit him two and sometimes three times a week, reviewing the missionary discussions with him. And we prayed, individually and as a District, that we could find a way to bring him to the waters of baptism.

And then the proverbial bombshell dropped.

We visited the Inspector one evening and presented him with a discussion on the commandments. I went over the law of chastity with him. He already knew the law of chastity and was living it. Elder Hammond covered all the aspects of the Word of Wisdom with him. He was, of course, already living the Word of Wisdom. I then began to cover the law of tithing. Only moments into the subject, the Inspector stopped me.

"This," he announced solemnly, "is why I haven't joined the Church."

The scales suddenly dropped from my eyes, and I felt much like Elijah's servant, who had his eyes miraculously opened. Everything became clear to me now and I smote my trouser leg understandingly. Tithing! Tithing is the issue that has kept him out of the Church for twenty years now. Why hadn't I seen this coming? It always seems to be either a concern with the Word of Wisdom or it's tithing. How had I not realized this sooner?

"You see," he continued. "My wife belongs to another church, and she would never allow me to give ten percent of my income to the Church of Jesus Christ. And I could never in good faith join the Church, any church for that matter, unless I am willing to live by all the ordinances, which is why I never joined the Church of Jesus Christ of Latter-day Saints."

Elder Hammond and I sat fermenting as a massive, stullen silence throbbed in the Inspector's tiny office.

- 61 -

This Takes the Cake

Elder Hammond and I unenthusiastically rehearsed the rest of the discussion with the Inspector, ended with a prayer, and then stepped out into the cold, quiet streets of Villa Mercedes. The night air smelled of petrichor from an approaching rain storm. We hurpled against the chilling wind as we walked in dazed silence toward our home. Our mood was sullen and somber.

"I knew it," I announced, managing finally to get the tongue unhinged and breaking the silence between us. "I knew there had to be something keeping him out of the Church all these years."

Elder Hammond said nothing.

"Tithing. I should've guessed it," I continued. "Twenty years investigating the Church, all those missionaries working with him. I just knew there had to be something. Tithing gets 'em every time."

After I had finished my rant, another rather strained and haughty silence ensued between us.

I must admit, I was feeling a bit lofty as if I had just beaten Hammond at a game of chess. How foolish the poor farm boy had been to believe that we could change twenty years of history, that somehow, against all odds, we could succeed where so many other missionaries had failed. At least now Elder Hammond would give up his delusion that the Inspector was a golden contact, and we could, in the short time we had remaining, concentrate on proselyting some other lost soul who desperately needed and was actively seeking the blessings of the restored gospel.

"I guess we'll be scratching the Inspector off our list of potential baptisms," I remarked after we arrived back at the apartment.

"Not at all," Hammond responded.

I did not understand.

"When you say, 'Not at all', don't you actually mean, 'Shucks, I guess so'?"

"Not at all. I mean we need to make another appointment with him," Elder Hammond proclaimed emphatically.

"Are you kidding?" I asked.

"Not at all," Hammond replied.

"Well, whatever for?" I asked, slightly bumfuzzled. "He just told us he won't join the Church. It's the same thing he's been telling missionaries for twenty years."

"I think we should see him on Tuesday."

"What's the point?" I asked.

"Well," Elder Hammond offered, "we still have one more discussion to cover with him. Any objections to that?"

"Shucks, not at all, I guess," I sourly surrendered.

It seemed like a tremendous waste of time to continue teaching the Inspector when we both knew he would never join the Church. Still, in the end, we really had nothing else constructive to do with our remaining days. I wasn't particularly against visiting the Inspector, especially when so few other investigators were vying for our attention and teachings. Still, if only on principle alone, I opposed it, and Elder Hammond knew it. It seemed the more I tried to avoid wasting our time teaching someone who had dodged, ducked, and eluded the waters of baptism for over twenty years, Elder Hammond would, all the more, devise opportunities for us to drop by and visit him. It became an unspoken point of contention between us.

In relating this tale, I may be conveying to you the notion that I did not love my companion with that special *philos* or brotherly love so familiar among the Lord's servants like Moses and Aaron, Joseph and Hyrum, or Jared and Mahonri Moriancumer. Nothing could be farther from the truth, or is it further? I did love Elder Hammond the same as I loved all my companions, but the notion that two young men can be thrown together and see everything eye-to-eye is being a little economical with the truth.

My first companion resented me before he even met me. He was finishing his mission in three weeks and wanted to go out with a bang. When he was told he would be getting an inexperienced 'greenie' for a companion, he immediately resented the idea that his new companion wouldn't be proficient in either the Spanish language or have a working knowledge of the missionary discussions. He lightened up a little after meeting me and learning that I had been speaking Spanish since I was thirteen years old and that I had memorized all the missionary discussions prior to leaving the MTC, thanks mostly to a girlfriend (who is now my wife) who would only go out with me if we studied the missionary discussions together before each date.

My second companion, a robust cowboy from Wyoming, for reasons unknown, disliked the Argentine people in general. He frequently badmouthed them, their customs, their language, and anything else he could imagine about them. He also didn't understand why I seemed to rail against him until our District Leader informed him that my mother was born and bred in Argentina and that I took every one of his insults against the Argentine people as a personal insult against my mother.

My third companion was one of those who had gone on a mission to find his testimony. He went because it was expected of him, and not because he had a burning desire to serve. Ironically, he was from Sacramento, California, not from Utah.

My fourth companion and I got along fine until I was called to serve as the District Leader in Rio Cuarto. He seemed, well, disconcerted is a word that comes to mind, by the fact that I had received the calling instead of him, and he literally stopped speaking to me for two weeks.

My point is that I loved all my companions, including Elder Hammond, but this brotherly affection did not preclude us from having difficulties and differences in our companionships. I have no doubt that even Mahonri Moriancumer resented being known only as the brother of Jared and not by his own good name.

Because of my great affection for Elder Hammond, I felt it was my duty to point out the futility of his efforts in getting the Inspector to take the plunge, figuratively speaking. I felt quite strongly that it was high time for some in-the-bud-type nipping. However, I knew I had to approach the subject delicately and with just the right amount of caution and finesse.

"You know Hammond, this is just a bunch of nonsense," I announced after dinner that evening. That was about all the finesse I could muster.

Hammond looked up from whichever one of Paul's epistles he was studying. "I'm sorry, Wylson. I didn't quite catch that. What were you talking nonsense about?"

"I wasn't talking nonsense."

"Oh, I thought you said you were."

"No. I said that all this business with the Inspector was a bunch of nonsense."

"How so?"

"Well, in case you haven't noticed, he's…, well, he's…, what's the word I'm looking for?"

"I have no idea what word you're looking for," Hammond indicated, rather bluntly, I might add. I have often heard of people who ground their heels into the carpet and, except for the fact that we didn't have a carpet, this is exactly what Hammond seemed to be doing.

"Well, he's… I mean, well…, you're never going to get the Inspector baptized!" I announced strongly.

There. I said it.

I could sense that Hammond, if not entirely disgruntled, was far from being gruntled.

"Why not?" he asked.

"Look, missionaries have been trying to baptize him for twenty years," I explained. "That's practically as long as you and I have been alive and they have all been unsuccessful. What makes you think we're going to change his mind?"

"I'm not trying to change his mind," Hammond replied with a sort of a whachamacallit in his voice.

"Then why do we keep going back?"

"Because I'm hoping the Spirit will change his heart."

Hammond quite literally reminded me of the Old Testament story of Balaam's ass. He seemed to be digging his heels in and refusing to listen to reason. Although I can't be certain, I think he might have even drawn his ears back a little in defiance.

"And I'm sure every missionary before us hoped and prayed for the same thing," I insisted, "but it never happened, and I don't see any reason why it's going to happen now."

"Ah," replied Hammond.

The exclamation of 'Ah' is a difficult one to argue with. 'Ah' is one of 109 allowable two-letter words in the game of Scrabble® and could indicate anything from delight to pain, surprise to complaint, pity to regret, or relief to contempt. It was anyone's guess which meaning Hammond intended.

I began to sense that laying out the truth was not working on my companion. Even less perspicacious minds than my own could detect that Hammond was not going to budge from his position.

The tension between Elder Hammond and I escalated over the next couple of days. As quiet as my companion had been during the first few weeks we had served together, he grew even more hushed. We walked the streets of Villa Mercedes mostly in silence. Back at the apartment, we studied the scriptures independently without speaking much. And we had entirely stopped talking about the Inspector.

On Tuesday, five days after the Inspector announced that he couldn't pay tithing and, therefore, wouldn't be joining the Church, Elder Hammond decided we should drop by and visit him. Spending more time with the Inspector seemed pointless, but it seemed even more meaningless to attempt to convince Hammond of that fact. I silently acquiesced, but it would be paltering with the truth to pretend that I was in any way gruntled about it.

Our Tuesday evening visit with the Inspector was pleasant but unproductive. We went over the final discussion with him, explaining the Priesthood and its purpose and power. The Inspector accepted every point we presented. But any progress toward baptism seemed not only improbable but impossible.

His stance on paying his tithing had not changed, and his conviction to not join the Church unless he could obey all the principles and ordinances was unwavering. We hadn't even seen his wife since that first day she almost devoured us on their doorstep, but we were convinced that she remained hostile toward the missionaries. Now that we had covered all six discussions with the Inspector, I imagined we would bid him farewell, as so many missionaries had done before us. It was a sad but inevitable conclusion.

I had developed a fondness for the comical Inspector. A missionary will rejoice over just being permitted into someone's home to share the gospel message. So often, potential investigators will listen with no real interest in exploring, grasping, or converting to the gospel. It was, therefore, a pleasure and a delight to discuss the restored gospel in depth with someone genuinely interested. But we had reached an impasse with the Inspector, and it was now time to move on.

Wednesday morning, after breakfast, prayers, and scripture study, I asked Elder Hammond:

"What are our plans for today then?"

"We're going to visit Sister Giuliano," Hammond told me.

"Sister Giuliano?" I asked, mostly out of curiosity.

"Yes," Hammond replied curtly.

"The Relief Society President?" I asked.

"Yes."

I couldn't help but wonder what business we had visiting the Relief Society President first thing on a Wednesday morning, but I didn't pursue the issue. It wasn't as if Hammond were trying to cozen me, in the words of the prolific author Iris Murdoch, "with a golden shrewdness." He just wasn't telling me what was going on. At least we appeared to be moving beyond wasting valuable proselyting time with the Inspector.

We knocked on the door of the Relief Society President shortly after nine a.m. She answered and seemed pleased that we had stopped by to visit her. Latin folk, I have found, are generally very gracious and hospitable toward visitors.

"Good morning," she announced enthusiastically. "What can I do for you, Elders?"

I, of course, didn't have a clue what she could do for us, so I let Elder Hammond speak.

"We are teaching an investigator and we would love it if you could bake her a cake and deliver it to her this evening."

This came as a complete surprise to me. I didn't know that we had another investigator. Then it disappointingly dawned on me; Hammond was referring to the Inspector's wife.

"I've written her name and address on the back of this card." He handed Sister Giuliano one of his missionary business cards, like the ones on which he had been writing scriptures every afternoon. "Can you do this for us, please?"

Her countenance changed from delighted to miffed, as she took the card and looked it over. I sensed that she was not thrilled with our request. After looking at the card for several seconds, she handed it back to Elder Hammond. Her demeanor was now somewhat discomposed.

"I don't have time to bake cakes today," she announced. "I can't just stop everything I'm doing to make a cake for someone. Perhaps some other time, or maybe you can find someone else who can do it, but you should let someone know in advance, not all spur of the moment like this."

Elder Hammond took back his little card and graciously thanked the Relief Society President as she closed the door on us. I could see from the look on Elder Hammond's face that he was deeply disappointed. I thought I may have actually felt a twinge of sympathy for the poor chump. He was trying so hard and had such dedication to what was, unfortunately, a lost cause. Still, Hammond apparently just wouldn't admit defeat.

When the Relief Society President had closed the door, and Hammond had tucked his little card back into his shirt pocket, I asked:

"Okay. Now what?"

"We are going to the store," Hammond firmly announced.

The shock this statement sent through me was second only to learning that Elder Hammond had a sense of humor. Missionaries are allowed one day to go shopping, do laundry, write letters home, and do other personal activities. It is called P-day; the P stands for 'preparation' or 'personal' or perhaps some other P word. For us, that day was Friday. We didn't need to do any shopping. We had all the food and toiletries we required back at the apartment, and what Hammond was planning was a direct and outright violation of a strict mission rule.

From all that I had gathered about Elder Hammond in our few weeks together, I noticed that he had been a real stickler for obedience to rules his entire time in the mission field. Why, I had to wonder, three weeks before being released and heading home to the farm, would he abandon his deep convictions and recklessly run off to the market? Still, it was Hammond's week to plan our schedule, and he was in charge, so I obediently followed his descent into disobedience.

I needed nothing from the market, so I simply followed Hammond around the store as he grabbed a few items from the shelves. Then, we headed back to the apartment. Hammond began unloading his purchases on the kitchen table. I was feeling somewhat disordered by the day's turn of events.

"So, now what are we doing?" I asked with perhaps a little more annoyance in my voice than I cared to portray.

"I'm going to bake a cake," Hammond revealed.

The day was simply not progressing in any way I could have imagined, and since Hammond, in his understandable disappointment at being wrong about the Inspector, was being less than communicative with me, I decided that it would be best just to roll with the punches and let Hammond do whatever he felt like doing.

"Well then," I said, "I'm going to the bedroom to study."

I lay down on my bed and, opening my triple combination, laid it firmly across my chest, closed my eyes, and proceeded to take an early but much-longed-for *siesta*. Some punches are just easier to roll with than others.

I woke to the smell of cake baking in the oven and the sight of Hammond sitting on the side of his bed, scriptures open in his lap while he copied more verses from Paul onto the backs of his missionary business cards.

"Hmmm," I said. "I must have fallen asleep."

I sat up, leaning against my headboard, and began reading about the two thousand stripling warriors who fought valiantly for the cause of the Nephites because they didn't doubt their mothers knew it. I looked over at Elder Hammond and began to wonder what his mother was like. I had no doubt Hammond's mother also knew it. Was she the one who taught him how to bake a cake from scratch? Was it his father who counseled him, perhaps as they stood on the edge of the south forty surveying the devastation left by a Kansas tornado, to never give up even in the face of overwhelming disaster, destruction, and disappointment?

I realized that I actually knew nothing about Elder Hammond's personal life other than the fact that he was fascinated by the writings of Paul. He was just a simple, quiet, humble kid, but he was also determined and dedicated. He had no delusions of grandeur, just a desire to serve. Perhaps more than any missionary I had ever met, Elder Hammond had a purity of spirit and an altruistic motivation in ministering. I pitied him. I think he actually believed he could make a difference with the Inspector. He held fastidiously to the faith that he could succeed where, for twenty-some-odd years, every missionary before him had failed.

After the cake had come out of the oven and cooled and Hammond had frosted it, I anticipated we'd visit the Inspector's home again. But, on this point, I was mistaken. Instead, we carried the cake over to the Relief Society President's home. When she answered the door, Hammond announced:

"I baked this cake for our investigator. We would really appreciate it if you could deliver it to her this evening. Would you be willing to do that?"

Sister Giuliano looked astonished, or do I mean astounded? I seemed to perceive a twinge of guilt sweep over her as she took the cake and agreed to deliver it to the Inspector's wife that evening.

"There's no need to tell her that I baked the cake. Just tell her it's from you," advised Elder Hammond. Here again, Hammond's perspicacity astounded me, or do I mean astonished? The cake would suggest so much more to the Inspector's wife if it were presented to her by a member of the Branch, someone from her own neighborhood, instead of by the missionaries.

The rest of the day and most of the following unfolded without incident. There were no more deviations from the strait and narrow path into inappropriate shopping excursions, no more slinking into the forbidden recesses of the marketplace on a non-P-day. And certainly, no more sitting at home baking cakes while the rest of the world was starving for the message of salvation that we were assigned to impart to them.

We knocked on a number of doors and held a few discussions with the mildly interested people we encountered at home. In other words, we led an average missionary's life. We knew we were coming down to the wire, so to speak. The entire District sensed that transfers were eminent and, in the air, as they say. We had determined that since Elder Hammond had arrived in Villa Mercedes a couple of days before me, he would likely be the one who would be transferred. Since Elder Price was the District Leader and still had about six months left on his mission, it only made sense that Elder Phillips would also be leaving soon. They had continued teaching the young lady they had met earlier, and although she was receptive, she seemed no closer to being baptized than the Inspector. It was anyone's guess which of the Sister Missionaries would be transferred. The winds of change were blowing strong in our little District.

Whatever our District Leader, Elder Price, had initially thought about the greatest, most experienced missionaries in the mission field performing miraculous mass conversions, none of us had had any success in bringing a single lost sheep into the fold. We spent most of our time knocking on doors. We worked with the members whenever we could and taught a few families but rarely were we invited back for a second discussion. All our efforts so far had been fruitless, but I was about to discover what a difference a cake makes.

On Thursday evening, Elder Hammond told me he wanted to stop by and visit the Inspector. I felt the old brow start to furrow.

"Why?" I asked. "We've taught him all the discussions."

"I just want to see how he's doing."

"He's doing the same as he's been doing for the past month. He loves the Church but he's not getting baptized. I thought he made that rather clear to us."

"Well, I want to see if his wife got the cake."

"His wife? His wife won't even open the door for us, Elder. What do expect is going to happen?"

"I dunno," Hammond replied.

I stared at him, astounded. I uttered no verbal retort but there was a distinct tsk in my gaze.

Neither of us said anything more.

We arrived at the Inspector's house, and Elder Hammond pounded on the massive wooden door. The Inspector's wife answered moments later. Physically, I probably didn't move, but my spirit recoiled at the sight of her. She must not have realized who was at the door since we hadn't made an appointment to visit that evening. I expected the door to fly shut, but to my absolute amazement, the Inspector's wife held the door open for us.

"*Pasen,*" she offered.

Had I heard correctly? She was asking us in? The lioness was inviting us into her den?

I was astonished—or, maybe, astounded. It's difficult to determine these things with the English language.

"Thank you, *Señora,*" the farm boy said as the Inspector's wife toddled off to another room. We found the Inspector in his office sitting at his desk.

"Your wife invited us in," Elder Hammond told the Inspector. He greeted us and, standing, he motioned for us to sit.

"*Sientense.* Sit, please."

"How are you doing?" Elder Hammond asked.

"Fine. Did you know a woman from your Church brought my wife a cake last night?"

"Well, that was nice," Elder Hammond replied.

"Yes. She stayed and visited a short while, too. They seemed to have a pleasant chat."

"That's good. I'm glad," said Hammond.

"I think it meant a lot to her," the Inspector added almost emotionally.

I was beginning to feel ashamed that I had not been more involved in the cake-baking project, but in my own defense, Hammond had never really shared with me any details of his culinary stratagem. It's a fine thing, just leaving me out in the cold like that!

After the initial and customary small talk, the Inspector finally asked what the purpose of our visit was this evening, something that I was interested in knowing myself. Had Hammond come to his senses and dropped by to say a final farewell to the Inspector? Did he want to bear one last testimony of the truthfulness of the gospel message before we abandoned the Inspector's soul to the wiles of the adversary? Was he finally ready to acknowledge that the Inspector was probably using tithing as an excuse to not join the Church and that he had no real interest in becoming a member?

Apparently not.

"We're having a baptism this Saturday," Elder Hammond announced. "We wanted to know if you could attend."

Again, I was stunned, or, possibly, stupefied. I hadn't heard of any baptisms planned for this Saturday. Had Elders Price and Phillips finally convinced their college-aged young lady to join the Church? No, it must have been the Sister Missionaries. Did they have someone prepared for baptism that I hadn't heard about? And when did Elder

Hammond find out about it since we were never apart?

"Well," remarked the Inspector, "who's getting baptized?"

I was asking myself the very same question.

Looking directly into the Inspector's eyes, Elder Hammond said matter-of-factly: "You are."

The Inspector lowered his head, and one of those long silences that people refer to as being pregnant ensued. The room remained quiet for several seconds before the Inspector delivered his response.

"I've told you already that I can't pay my tithing," the Inspector replied.

Elder Hammond leaned forward in his chair.

"*Señor* Navarro," he said with marked determination, "God doesn't care about your tithing. He wants you to be baptized. If you'll get baptized, God will take care of your tithing."

My mind started reeling. How could you say that to someone? All members are asked to pay tithing. You can't tell someone

God doesn't care about their tithing just because you want them to get baptized. That's why we teach the discussions, to let people know what the gospel consists of and what is expected of them as members of Christ's Church. God's not going to make an exception for the Inspector.

"What time is the baptism?" asked the reluctant Inspector.

"It's at one in the afternoon," Elder Hammond replied, getting to his feet. "Will you be there?"

I took my cue and stood up beside Elder Hammond.

"Well, yeah. I guess I can make it," said the Inspector.

"Good," said Elder Hammond. "And invite your wife to come, too. Will you?"

"Yeah. Sure," replied the Inspector, with more than a hint of uncertainty in his voice.

He escorted us to the front door.

"Okay, we'll see you Saturday at one," Hammond stated more than asked. "And don't forget to invite your wife."

"No, I won't forget."

On our way home, we stopped by the Branch President's house to inform him that there would be a baptism on Saturday. Then, we visited Elders Price and Phillips to let them know.

After prayers that night, I climbed into bed, but I didn't fall sleep right away. I kept thinking about how many missionaries had visited and taught the Inspector. How many had felt like he was their golden contact in the beginning, only to be disappointed and abandon their efforts when he announced he couldn't pay tithing? Dozens perhaps had taught him and prayed with him and for him. Eventually, all of them, at one point or another, had given up on him, me included.

It seemed that none of us could move beyond the notion that the Inspector, although willing, insisted he couldn't pay tithing. And all of us had, in turn, borne our testimonies and moved on. Elder Hammond saw a clearer purpose to his mission and calling. He trusted in the Lord and the promise made through Nephi. He understood that if the Inspector would simply go and do the things the Lord commanded, then the Lord would prepare a way for him to accomplish the thing which he commanded.

My perception of Elder Hammond as a naive country bumpkin changed dramatically that evening. My faith apparently did not.

Setting the Town on Fire

Did I mention that our landlady has a dog? I should have. It's a scruffy old thing who seems to think he's the ruler of the entire house. He is a mix of breeds—part terrier, part who-knows-what?—but his infectious energy makes up for any lack of pedigree. His fur is a chaotic blend of brown and grey patches that look like they were splashed on haphazardly by some unskilled painter. Despite his rugged appearance, there's something you'd almost called endearing about him. Maybe it's how he wags his tail with such vigor that his whole body shakes or how his big, round eyes make him appear so sad and pitiful.

The day before the baptism was Friday, our P-day, as I mentioned earlier. Elder Hammond and I had gone out to do our weekly grocery shopping. After we had returned home and properly placed our purchases in their appropriate places in the kitchen, we went into the bedroom only to find the landlady's hound hunkered down on my bed, the only other bed in the room that wasn't Hammond's.

I approached the bed and, leaning down, began to pet the miserable mongrel on the top of its head, which consequently positioned my face very close to the pooch's proboscis. I warmly whispered, "Who's a good doggy, then?"

The canine in question responded by lunging forward, snapping at my face, and splitting my upper lip from the nasal septum to the tubercle of the upper lip, and then running off with its tail between its legs. This was somewhat unnerving. I quickly grabbed the handkerchief my mother had insisted I take with me from the top drawer of my dresser and attempted to stop the flow of blood.

Hammond asked to see the injury.

"That's gonna need stitches," he calmly announced.

I responded by saying, "Grae. Huhmm ugh sufugh u-vay frr ud?"

"You don't have to pay for it," Hammond replied. "Argentina has socialized medicine."

"Ueg oose?" I asked.

"Yes, it does. Now let's get you to the hospital."

At the hospital, I was ushered into a small room and told to wait for the doctor. I hoped someone would show up before the *siesta* started, and I was in luck. Two doctors came in to see me and examined my lip.

"We're going to need to stitch that," stated the first doctor.

I nodded in agreement as the two medical professionals began gathering the tools of their specialized trade.

"You know," asserted the second doctor after they had placed their operating instruments on the metal tray beside the bed on which I was sitting, "if we give you a shot with a needle to deaden the pain, that will be the same as if we just sew you up with the needle. So, we'll just skip the anesthesia."

"Vud?" I exclaimed.

But before the second doctor could answer, the first doctor had threaded a needle and proceeded to stitch together my upper lip *sans* any artificially induced loss of ability to feel agony during the performance of surgery.

I left the hospital with more pain than I had when I entered it. The gauze bandage I was now sporting firmly across my upper lip resembled a Charlie Chaplin mustache. "So, that's pretty cool," I thought.

"Wow," exclaimed Hammond on the way home. "I can't believe they sewed you up without giving you any anesthesia. That must have been painful."

I sensed that, on some level, he might have enjoyed watching me go through that excruciating experience.

"Yeah," I replied. "Socialized medicine. Isn't it wonderful?"

"So, are you gonna feel up to chopping wood tomorrow?" Hammond asked.

"Yes, Elder," I answered with a heavy sigh. "I'm still planning on chopping wood."

The chapel in Villa Mercedes is a small, rented home across from the plaza. The dining room serves as a makeshift foyer, and the living room is the chapel. Folding metal chairs are set up in neat rows facing a movable podium. A foot pedal organ sits in the corner with a metal music stand beside it. The classrooms are converted bedrooms with rows of folding chairs as well. The building has no baptismal font, so missionaries, long before my time, built an above-ground font against a side wall in the outdoor patio. Here, a most significant event was about to occur—the baptism of a new member into the Church of Jesus Christ of Latter-day Saints.

Since no one had installed plumbing to the font, a garden hose was attached to the kitchen faucet, fed out through a window, and then stretched across the courtyard. This was the method used for filling the font, a process that took about four hours.

Did I mention that the building had no hot water?

The building had no hot water. During the colder months, water for baptisms was heated by filling two fifty-five-gallon metal drums placed on grills next to the font and subsequently building a fire underneath them.

Early in the morning on the Saturday of the baptism, the Sister Missionaries, along with the Branch President, busied themselves with the tasks of filling the font and arranging the chairs in the courtyard. Elders Price,

Phillips, Hammond, and I headed to the outskirts of town, to a densely forested area. Of course, the short walk was replete with wisecracks about the bandage above my upper lip. Elder Price waddled around me like Charlie Chaplin. Elder Phillips clicked his heels together, shot a stiff arm in the air, and 'heiled' me. Boys can be so immature.

When we reached the woods, we searched for and gathered large branches of fallen timber and dragged them through the streets of Villa Mercedes back to the little chapel in front of the plaza. It took several trips to bring in enough wood to heat the fifty-five-gallon drums. And yes, this was done in white shirts and ties.

By the time we brought in the necessary firewood, the two drums had been filled, and the hose had been placed in the font to fill it. The Branch President excused himself for the morning, and Elders Price, Phillips, and the two Sisters took off to do their regular missionary service. Elder Hammond and I remained at the chapel and took turns chopping the firewood. The remainder of the morning was spent building and stoking the fire.

At the right moment, just prior to the candidate entering the font, we would don heavy leather gloves and, lifting the barrels of hot water, dump them into the font. To be perfectly honest, the two fifty-five-gallon drums only served to take the chill off the icy water that filled the font, making its temperature overall almost tolerable. As I stood there, hands trembling from the cold, I couldn't help but reflect on the significance of this baptism and the challenges we had overcome to make it happen.

Shadrach, Meshach, and Abednego may have emerged from their fiery furnace unsinged and not even smelling of smoke, but by one o'clock on Saturday afternoon, Elder Hammond and I smelled like we'd been on a two-week Boy Scout campout in the North Woods. The other two Elders and the Sisters had returned. The Branch President returned, and several of the faithful members of the Branch also showed up to witness the Inspector's baptism. Only one thing was missing, of course; the Inspector himself.

The skies were overcast. The air was quiet and cold. The members stood around shivering and conversing with the Sisters while the Elders and I continued to feed the fire. No one seemed overly concerned that we may be doing all this for nothing.

The Argentine people are very dear to my heart—as I mentioned, my mother is one of them—but they give new meaning to the term "fashionably late." If you think ten or fifteen minutes is fashionable, then you obviously haven't attended a church meeting in South America.

My father once pontificated on the differences between the Spanish language and culture and those of his native English. While Americans are fast-paced, on-the-go people, he told me, the people of South America are easy-going and, shall we say, slow? In English, we have expressions like, "Is your refrigerator running?" In contrast, in Spanish, the expression translates as "Is your refrigerator walking?"

This led him to ponder whether the people of South America were slow because their language was slow or the language was slow because the people were slow. If he ever discovered the truth of whether culture creates the language or language establishes the culture, it is a secret he has carried with him to the grave. In any case, it was half past one, and there was still no sign of the Inspector, neither walking nor running.

Some suggested that we go to his house to remind him that he had agreed to make a covenant with God today at one o'clock, not that a person should need to be reminded of such a substantial commitment. Perhaps they thought we should drag him kicking and screaming to the waters of baptism. It was, after all, for his own good. The one person who seemed immune to any concern over the Inspector's absence was Elder Hammond.

"Don't worry," Hammond would comment when the issue was brought up by some poor soul who was probably close to frostbite. "The Inspector will be here."

A quarter till two approached and departed without any sign of the prospective new member. The other members huddled against the cold, but no one went home. And then, precisely at two o'clock, the courtyard gate swung open to reveal Inspector Clouseau, I mean *Señor* Navarro, in his trench coat and hat, now ready to enter the waters of baptism and become a member of the Church of Jesus Christ of Latter-day Saints.

The Branch President rushed to help the Inspector into his white baptismal clothing, while the members of the Branch seemed to regain their enthusiasm and warmth. I suggested to Sister Campbell that we change the opening hymn from *Father in Heaven, We Do Believe* to *Smoke Gets in Your Eyes* by *The Platters.*

She was reluctant, probably because she didn't know all the words. As the Branch President and the Inspector stepped out into the courtyard clothed entirely in white, Elder Hammond and I put on thick leather gloves and hoisted the two heavy barrels, emptying the warm water into the font.

After a lengthy twenty-year journey, the Inspector entered the waters of baptism, received a remission of his sins, and joined the fold of Christ. This would be the final convert baptism of my two-year mission, and I really had nothing at all to do with it. Halfway through my mission, the Mission President gave us all a challenge to baptize twenty-five people while serving. The Inspector was my 28th baptism.

My father served as a missionary in Argentina three decades earlier; that is how he met my mother. During his two-and-a-half-year mission, he had only one convert baptism. He told me it was a day he would never forget. The entire Branch rented a bus and drove to a nearby river. A torrential rain fell the entire day. As the bus pulled up along the banks of the river, the clouds above their little group parted, and the sun poured down on them. Immediately after the baptism, the clouds closed again, and the rain returned.

Nothing so dramatic or spectacular occurred during the Inspector's baptism. We didn't have rain, but the sky remained gloomy, the air cold and biting, and in the little church courtyard, the grey smoke lingered. Despite all of this, the members were cheerful, and the Inspector seemed happy with the commitment he had finally accepted.

Amidst the enthusiasm, I sensed something put a damper on the afternoon for Elder Hammond. I had expected him to be overjoyed at the prospect of another baptism, which he was, but my keen intuitiveness warned me that something was not quite right.

As the Inspector went off to dry himself, Hammond turned to me and said, "I wish his wife could have been here."

I have occasionally had non-members of the Church of Jesus Christ express the viewpoint that it is wrong to send missionaries throughout the world to "force our beliefs on others." The surprising irony is that not only does the Church not "force" its beliefs or practices on others, it will not even accept a person for baptism who doesn't meet five particular criteria. Every candidate for baptism must:

1. Believe in God the Father and in His Son Jesus Christ,

2. have a testimony of the truthfulness of the Book of Mormon,

3. accept Joseph Smith as a prophet,

4. accept the current Presidency and Apostles as prophets, seers, and revelators,

5. and be willing to obey the commandments of God.

Technically, the Inspector met all five of these requirements. He was willing to pay tithing; his wife was preventing him. But, as I lay in bed that night, I wondered if we had really done the Inspector any good or had we just created another inactive member of the Church.

The Inspector was very clear that he would not be able to pay his tithing, yet he felt it was important to obey all commandments and ordinances. How many talks and lessons, I wondered, would he listen to on the topic of tithing? How many Priesthood leaders would counsel him that he needs to pay his tithing to receive the full blessings the Lord has for him before his guilt at not being obedient would drive him out of activity? I could envision him slowly withdrawing from the Church and eventually shutting himself off from all contact with the members or the missionaries.

"This is great," I said to myself as I finally fell asleep. "We've just added another inactive member to the rolls of the Church."

Although my companion deserves all the credit, I found little satisfaction in the fact that Elder Hammond and I were the missionaries who finally brought the Inspector to the waters of baptism.

- 101 -

Out for a Walk

Sunday morning dawned cold and bitter as Hammond and I made our way to the chapel. The sky was slate-grey, thick with threatening clouds. An icy wind whipped through the narrow streets as our steps sounded off the old cobblestones. Hammond showed no outward signs of exuberance over yesterday's events, but the tension between us seemed to have dissipated.

"Do you think we did the right thing, Elder?" I asked as we plodded together toward the chapel.

"Whada'ya mean?" Hammond replied.

"I mean, baptizing a guy who can't, or won't, pay his tithing?"

"It'll be fine," he assured me.

"How could it be?" I asked. "Don't you think guilt is going to overtake him one day and force him into inactivity?"

"I doubt it."

"I think he's going to keep hearing about tithing, and his conscience is going to eat away at him until he just stops going to church."

"Does your conscience eat away at you?" Hammond asked.

"Well, no, but I pay my tithing."

"We all have something though," Hammond added.

"Yeah, but not as big as tithing. Tithing is big," I declared.

"The Apostle Paul says that a small sin will keep you out of Heaven just the same as a big one."

I could argue with Hammond, but I couldn't argue with the Apostle Paul.

As we arrived at the Church, the members began filing into the foyer/dining room of the small building, the women heading for the chapel/living room for Relief Society and the men heading for one of the converted classrooms for Priesthood meeting. We had reminded the Inspector at his baptism that Church began promptly at nine on Sunday morning, although nine-ten would be closer to the truth, and we were pleased to see him walk through the door on time. Of course, he came without his wife, but I had already expected that. As I explained the order of events to him, he reached into the pocket of his overcoat and removed a standard white envelope, which he then presented to me.

"What's this?" I asked.

"That is my tithing," the Inspector casually replied.

I was stunned. The Inspector's revelation hit me like a freight train crashing through my perceptions, leaving everything in disarray. It wasn't just the shock of the revelation itself; it was the weight of its implications—how everything I thought I knew was suddenly called into question. Each shameful skepticism, once a sturdy pillar in my cynical mind's architecture, began to crumble under the unseen force of this miraculous moment. I found myself standing at the precipice of uncertainty, staring down into an abyss where answers should have been. What if every encounter I'd dismissed as uninterested or even unwilling had held deeper potential? What if each casual contact I took for granted danced along that thin line between ordinary and—I dread to say it—golden?

Realizing that standing there frozen wouldn't move the situation any further along, I forced myself to breathe deeply, then added:

"I thought you said you couldn't pay tithing."

"Well, that's a funny story," said the Inspector. "You see, when I left my house yesterday to come to the baptism, I didn't actually tell my wife what I was doing."

"Ah," I said, indicating surprise and amazement.

"No. I told her that I was just going out for a walk. Well, as you can imagine, she didn't believe me, and she was concerned."

"Of course," I interjected, indicating that I could very well imagine and even understood her concern perfectly.

"Right. So, after I left the house, she went to the bedroom to pray."

"She did what now?" I asked.

"She prayed, and while she was praying, the Lord told her that I hadn't gone for a walk but that I had gone to the Church of Jesus Christ of Latter-day Saints and that I was taking an important step in that Church. He told her that it would be alright. So, there you have it," he added, looking down at the standard white envelope I held in my hands. "That is my tithing."

"She did what?" I asked again, still somewhat stupefied.

"She prayed and the Lord told her it was alright." He paused, perhaps to ensure that I had caught the gist of his words this time. "So, there's my tithing."

"What? Just like that?"

"Yes, Elder Wylson. Just like that."

I took the Inspector to the Branch President and had him deliver the standard white envelope and its contents to him while I went to find Elder Hammond. He was already seated in Priesthood meeting, which had somehow started without me. I took the vacant seat next to my companion, then leaned in and whispered:

"The Inspector just handed me something."

No reaction. Hammond sat motionless, staring ahead at the Elders' Quorum President, who was detailing the announcements for the upcoming week.

"It was his tithing," I told him with a whisper of amazement.

Not even the twitch of an eyebrow appeared on my unresponsive companion. This was not the rejoinder you would expect from someone when being told about a minor miracle of this caliber. Perhaps I simply needed to jog Hammond's memory a tad.

"Remember, he told us he couldn't pay his tithing?"

Hammond remained motionless and statuesque.

"You know, 'cause of his wife and all."

Still no response.

"Well, he just paid his tithing after all. Pretty cool, I'd say."

And there it was! Barely perceptible, just a hint actually, but something had registered somewhere within the deep recesses of my stoic companion's soul as I perceived the tiniest return of that farm boy grin. It was like watching the sun burst through a thick layer of storm clouds, bringing light to the surrounding shadows, or something like that.

- 109 -

Talents and Transfers

Most of the following week was uneventful. At the next District meeting, Elder Price congratulated Hammond and me on our baptism. He also announced that the Branch was having a social get-together on Saturday evening and that the missionaries should spend the week inviting non- and less-active members to attend. The event was a talent show, a unique opportunity for us to connect with the community. Of course, we would be expected to perform whatever talent we possessed.

I don't sing. I don't play a musical instrument. I certainly don't dance. My biggest talent is that I can flawlessly recite *The Cremation of Sam McGee,* a lengthy poem written by Robert W. Service.

When I was thirteen, Elder Bruce R. McConkie visited our area, and my parents invited him for dinner. Elder McConkie was not only tall and stern, but he was also terrifying and fearsome. As he reached out to shake my puny little hand, I felt he could see right into my heart and soul and knew every evil thing about me—the firecracker I had put in my sister's Barbie doll, the sixty-four pennies I had taken from my brother's coin collection to buy candy with, the name I had frequently called the kid who lived down the street—all passed before my eyes and I would fain have been glad to have commanded the rocks and the mountains to fall upon me to hide me from his presence. Instead, I just avoided making eye contact with him throughout dinner.

Halfway through the meal, however, my father turned to me. "Son," he said, "Why don't you recite *The Cremation of Sam McGee* for Elder McConkie?"

Having been put thusly on the spot as it were, I stood and began my recitation, not remembering the expletives that would need to be deleted from the narrative. You can only imagine the mortification I felt, a small, wimpy thirteen-year-old standing before this gigantic man of God, about to utter a profanity.

"He was always cold," I recited. "But the land of gold / Seemed to hold him like a spell.

"Though he'd often say, in his homely way, / That he'd sooner live in…"

Suddenly, it struck me! I was about to swear in front of a General Authority, and not just any General Authority, but Bruce R. McConkie, the largest, scariest, and most spiritually dynamic General Authority I knew. His stone-cold, piercing eyes bore into my soul, and I felt a stark fate approaching similar to that of Uzza after he steadied the Ark of the Covenant. I was toast!

I panicked, stammering. "That he'd…, that he'd…, he'd sooner live somewhere else," I declared.

Relief! Tragedy averted. Fire from the skies would not be falling on little Billy Wylson today.

Of course, *The Cremation of Sam McGee* would do me little good here in Villa Mercedes, as I only knew it in English. I continued to rack my brain for a talent I could share with the members of the Branch. And then, the proverbial lightning bolt struck.

In Argentina, there is really only one sport, and that is soccer. A few people play a little basketball, but in my experience, it's young members of the Church who play because the missionaries have taught them the game. American football is virtually unknown and baseball… well, baseball is just confusing.

I have no talent or ability in sports, but I had the idea that I could adapt and translate Abbott and Costello's *Who's on First* into a lesson on how to play the American game of baseball. I recruited Elder Price to be Costello.

"I'll write it up," I told him, "and we can rehearse it on P-day."

Early Friday morning, Hammond and I headed to Elders Price and Phillips's apartment to begin our rehearsal. When we arrived, we found a fly in the ointment, well, not literally, although it wasn't unusual to find a fly or a cockroach or some other creature in the ointment, or between the bed sheets or even in the food. In the area where I had started my mission, in a little town called *Posito*, the home where we stayed daily served us a warm, watery cabbage soup with little creatures that looked very similar to black pepper floating on top. But I digress.

The fly, as I have called it, was revealed by Elder Price.

"Transfers have come in," he stated.

"Transfers have come in?" I asked.

"Transfers have come in. Elder Phillips is going to Tucumán."

"Phillips is going to Tucumán?"

"Philips is going to Tucumán and Hammond is headed to Rio Cuarto."

"Hammond is headed to Rio Cuarto?"

"Yes, as soon as he can get packed and purchase bus fare."

"What about the Sisters?" I asked.

"What about the Sisters?" Elder Price countered.

"Well, that's what I'm asking. What about the Sisters?"

"They're both staying."

"They're both staying?" I asked, incredulous.

"Yes. They're going to finish their missions right here."

"So, who's going to train their replacements?"

"No one. They're not being replaced."

"They're not being replaced?"

"Not at this time."

"Oh!" I said, or some similar two-letter exclamation indicating incredulity and wonder.

We canceled rehearsals for the expertly adapted Spanish rendition of *Who's on First*, or, as we now called it, *Quien Esta en Primero?* and Hammond and I returned to our apartment so he could pack.

Later that morning, we checked the bus schedule, and Hammond bought himself a ticket for Saturday morning, and just like that, Elder Hammond was gone. Phillips left that same morning, and Elder Price and I threw in together to await our new companions, who arrived early Saturday afternoon.

In the interim, we rehearsed *Who's on First*.

Elder Price's new companion was a greenie. Mine may not have been green, but he wasn't fully ripe, either. Nonetheless, he would become the senior companion in about ten days when I went home.

Back at the apartment, I sat down on my bed, then pointed to the neat and meticulously made bed vacated by Hammond, the only other bed in the room that wasn't mine.

"That," I said to my new companion, pointing out the obvious, "is your bed."

While he unpacked, I told my new companion a little about the area we worked in, what the members were like, and who we had been teaching. I also told him about the talent show the Branch was holding that evening.

"So, I'll get to meet the members right off!" he mentioned, sounding somewhat overly eager and enthused. "Do we have a lot of families to teach?"

"Not really," I admitted. "At least, not any real serious ones."

"No golden contacts, huh?"

I shuddered. He continued: "Too bad. Have you had a lot of baptisms?"

"Well, I'm not one to brag but I've had my fair sh— Oh, you mean here in Villa Mercedes, don't you? Well, we just had one a week ago."

"Man! That's fantastic!"

"Yeah," I reminisced, wondering if reminiscing was even possible after just one week. "It was fantastic, miraculous even."

"So, was it an entire family?"

"What? Oh, no. No, just an elderly gentleman. You'll probably meet him tonight." Then I chuckled. "You know, he kind of looks like Inspector Clouseau."

"Really?" replied my new companion with less humor than I had anticipated.

"Well, not the Peter Seller's version of Clouseau, more like the cartoon version," I added.

The newbie, apparently unimpressed by the Inspector's similarity to a famous cartoon figure, tucked the last of his belongings in his drawer and shoved his now-empty suitcase under the bed.

"So, what have we got planned for this afternoon?" he over-anxiously bellowed, although bellowed may be overstating the point.

"Nothing," I replied. "We didn't know when you were coming."

"Oh. Right. Well, shall we go out and knock on a few doors then?" he asked.

"Sure." I sighed a perfectly audible sigh. "Why not?"

At the Branch talent show, I introduced my new companion to all the members. Apparently, the Inspector had stayed home. I hoped he'd at least make it to Church in the morning.

The Branch President conducted the program that evening. The young women performed a *Samba*, a traditional Argentine folk dance. One of the young men did an impersonation of Landresina, a celebrity comedian. Elders Price and Phillips had invited their college-aged contact to sing and perform a song on her guitar. She delivered a heart-rending performance of the Argentine folk song, *Quédate en Mi*, and I was sorry that Phillips wasn't there to hear it.

Finally, it was time for Elder Price and me to take the stage, the stage simply being the front of the room. I had brought an old chalkboard from one of the classrooms and drew a baseball diamond on it. Before going on stage, I carefully removed the white bandage from my lip and colored it with a black magic marker. Then I replaced it on my lip, making it look like I had grown a mustache. Boys can be so immature, I know.

On stage, I began explaining the game of baseball to Elder Price. The members were fascinated. Then we reached the part where I explained the player's nicknames.

"They give these ball players now-a-days very peculiar names," I began.

"You mean funny names?"

"…We have Who's on first, What's on second, I Don't Know is on third."

"You don't know the fellows' names?"

"Well, I should."

"Well, then, who's on first?"

"Yes."

"I mean the fellow's name."

"Who."

"The guy on first."

"Who."

"The first baseman."

"Who."

"The guy playing…"

"Who is on first!"

"I'm asking *you* who's on first."

"That's the man's name."

"That's who's name?"

"Yes."

The members had never heard of either Abbott or Costello and were literally eating this stuff up. Or do I mean figuratively?

"Well, go ahead and tell me."

"That's it."

"That's who?"

"Yes."

"Look, you got a first baseman?"

"Certainly."

"Who's playing first?"

"That's right."

"When you pay off the first baseman every month, who gets the money?"

"Every dollar of it."

I don't wish to bore you with reminiscences of my theatrical talents, but it was at about this point in our impeccable performance that I saw the foyer door open and watched the Inspector slip inside, fashionably late, and stand quietly at the back of the room.

"All I'm trying to find out is the fellow's name on first base," Elder Price continued.

"Who."

"The guy that gets…"

"That's it."

"Who gets the money…"

Looking back at the Inspector, I did a double-take and almost forgot my next line. He hadn't come alone.

"He does, every dollar. Sometimes his wife comes down and collects it."

"Who's wife?"

"Yes."

"All I'm trying to find out is what's the guy's name on first base?"

"No. What is on second base."

"I'm not asking you who's on second."

"Who's on first."

I could hardly believe my eyes. The Inspector had brought his wife, who was standing at his side in the back of the room.

"What's the guy's name on first base?"

"No. What is on second."

"I'm not asking you who's on second."

"Who's on first."

"I don't know."

"He's on third, we're not talking about him."

I wasn't the only one who noticed that the Inspector had actually convinced his wife to join him. The Relief Society President also saw the Inspector's wife enter the room. She stood up from her seat and welcomed her new friend with a warm hug. The two of them were inseparable the entire evening. The following morning, the Inspector brought his wife to Sunday services.

The trip from Buenos Aires to Los Angeles is about a thirteen-hour flight, which, as John Denver noted, is a long time to hang in the sky. Our group of thirteen Elders and now two Sisters grew a little stir-crazy as we soared through the air for hours. Luckily, the flight was not completely booked, and some of us could stretch out in the empty seats a bit. I read, played chess with Phillips, and walked about the plane conversing with other missionaries. I finally went and sat beside Elder Hammond. He was reading from the epistles of Paul.

"Looking forward to getting back to the farm?" I asked.

"Sure," he responded not looking up from his scriptures.

"You know, you never told me what kind of farm it is, but I had this great idea after you left."

"It's a wheat farm."

"It is?"

"Yes."

"Are you sure about that?"

"Yes."

"You sure it's not a chicken farm?"

"Nope. It's a wheat farm."

"Well, I guess you'd know best, but I had this great idea, if it were a chicken farm, you could call it Hammond Eggs."

"It's a wheat farm."

"I don't know. Hammond Wheat doesn't have the same ring to it, does it?"

"No. It doesn't."

"Well, I suggest when you get home and get all settled in, you should look into investing in chicken farming."

"I'll be sure to take that into consideration."

"I mean, you almost have to, what with a name like Hammond Eggs." I remarked.

"Yes, and then I guess we'd have to invest in some pigs as well," Hammond added somewhat sarcastically I'm thinking.

"Now you're talking!" I said, slapping him on the shoulder.

I started to get up, and then I remembered why I was seeking out Elder Hammond in the first place.

"So, do you know why I came back here to visit with you?" I asked.

"Let me see, ... to see if I could read your mind?"

"What? No. That would be ridiculous! I came back to tell you that the Inspector's wife came to the talent show. She showed up with the old guy."

"Did she?" he more stated than asked.

"She certainly did. Sister Giuliano went and sat with her. I think they're going to be friends."

I stood up again.

"Oh," I turned and added, "and she came to Church on Sunday."

With his nose still firmly set in the epistles, Hammond remained nonchalant and almost seemed unimpressed. There was no suggestion of surprise at this announcement of good news. Actually, I don't think he was surprised at all. I think he already knew. He had the faith to see it all right from the very beginning.

Elder Phillips and I parted ways at the Los Angeles International Airport, and even though he lives just up El Cajon Pass in Bakersfield, I never saw him again.

Elder Price returned home six months after Elder Hammond and me, and from what I understand, he went right to work on reclaiming his girlfriend. They were married about six months later.

A few years later, I heard through the grapevine that Sister Rogers had passed away sometime after returning to her home in Idaho.

I stuck around Los Angeles since that's where my family was now living, and I began teaching early morning Seminary in Redondo Beach. One of the techniques I taught my students for memorizing scriptures, one that I still use today, is to write the scripture on the back of a business card and carry it with them in a shirt pocket, taking it out whenever they have a spare moment to re-read it.

Elder Hammond went home to the farm in Kansas, and that was the last I ever heard of him, but the impression he left on me was indelible, if that's the word I want. He gave me one of the greatest lessons on faith and trust in God that I have ever learned. He, together with the Inspector, showed me what Nephi had taught about doing the things that the Lord commanded, and He shall prepare a way for them so that they may accomplish the thing which he commands them.

Occasionally, when I'm doing the grocery shopping, I still check to see if they have a carton of Hammond Eggs.

About the Author

Bill Wylson is the author of over 55 published works on family values, religious issues, and religious education. His work has appeared in The Ensign, This People, Liberty Magazine, Success, and many others.

Bill served a full-time mission in Cordoba, Argentina. He has also taught Seminary classes, Gospel Doctrine classes, Elders' Quorums, and High Priest Quorums. Bill has served in four Elders' Quorum presidencies, one High Priests' Group presidency, and two Bishoprics.

Bill Wylson currently lives in Salt Lake City, Utah.

9 798230 779131